This book belongs to:

Published by Ladybird Books Ltd
A Penguin Company
Penguin Books Ltd, 80 Strand, London WC2R 0RL, UK
Penguin Books Australia Ltd, Camberwell, Victoria, Australia
Penguin Books (NZ) Ltd, Private Bag, 102902, NSMC, Auckland 10, New Zealand

7 9 10 8

ISBN-13: 978-1-84422-279-7
ISBN-10: 1-84422-279-9

Printed in Italy

Baby Animals

written by Lorraine Horsley
illustrated by Sharon Harmer

Baby Animals

puppy

fawn

calf

fry

kid

A baby cat is a kitten.
When they are born,
kittens like to sleep with
their brothers and sisters.

How many kittens can you see?

A baby kangaroo is a joey. When they are born, joeys live in their mothers' pouches.

How many joeys can you see?

A baby lion is a cub. When they are born, cubs feed on their mother's milk.

How many cubs can you see?

A baby horse is a foal. When they are born, foals can walk.

horse
foal
How many foals can you see?

A baby bird is a chick.
When they are born,
chicks live in a nest
made by their parents.

How many chicks can you see?

A baby dog is a puppy.
When they are born,
puppies cannot see.

How many puppies can you see?

A baby deer is a fawn. When they are born, fawns hide in the grass to keep safe.

How many fawns can you see?

A baby elephant is a calf. When they are born, calves stay close to their mothers.

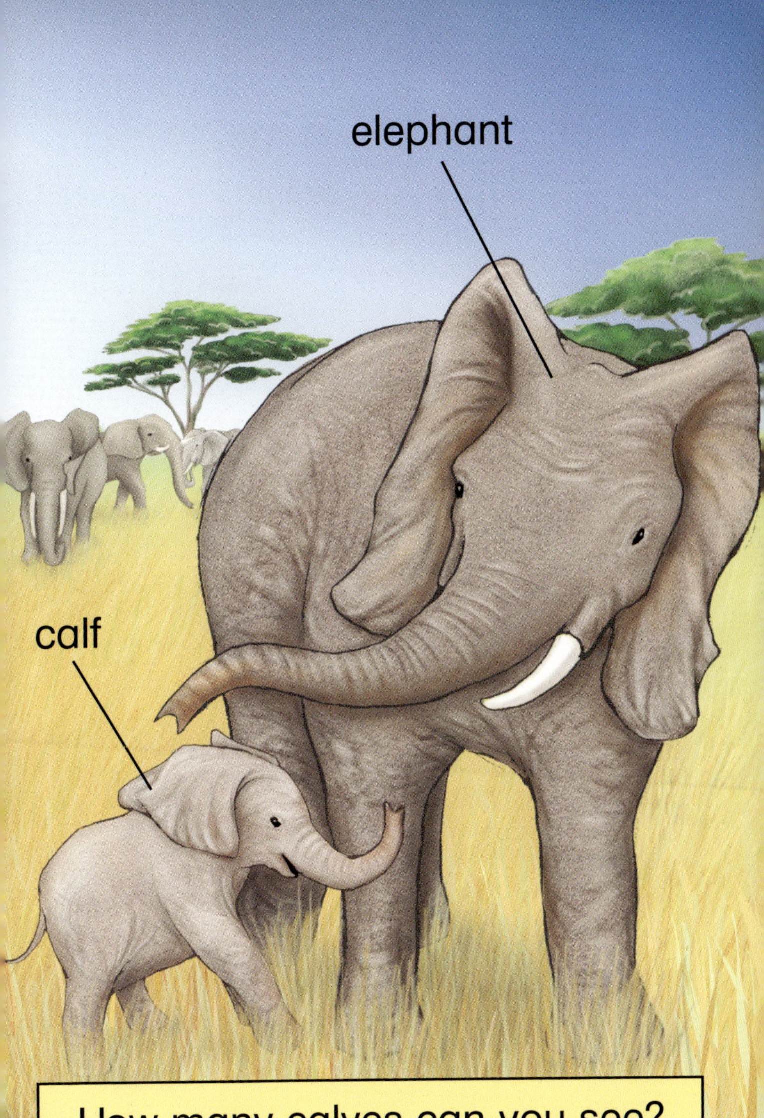

How many calves can you see?

A baby goat is a kid.
When they are born, kids
can climb steep mountains.

How many kids can you see?

Baby fish are fry.
When they are born, most fry have to look after themselves.

How many fry can you see?

These baby animals are all called cubs.

These baby animals are all called calves.

Index